Withdrawn

Yellowstone National Park

Nate Frisch

Published by
CREATIVE EDUCATION

P.O. Box 227, Mankato, Minnesota 56002
Creative Education is an imprint of The Creative Company
www.thecreativecompany.us

Design and production by Danny Nanos of Gilbert & Nanos
Art direction by Rita Marshall
Printed in the United States of America

Photographs by Getty Images (Kick Images), nps.gov, Shutterstock (And_Ant, Antonio Abrignani, akva, alessandro0770, Linda Armstrong, BL, Blue Ice, Sebastien Burel, Sascha Burkard, Colin Edwards Photography, creativex, Elizabeth C. Doerner, Dennis Donohue, Evgeny Dubinchuk, EastVillage Images, eye-for-photos, julius fekete, Maran Garai, gary718, gracious_tiger, Kenneth Keifer, Paul Knowles, John Kropewnicki, Geoffrey Kuchera, Julie Lubick, Stephanie Lupoli, maga, Rob Marmion, Mayskyphoto, Caitlin Mirra, pashabo, PFlynnPhoto, pix2go, Rambleon, Henryk Sadura, Schalke fotografie/Melissa Schalke, Daniel M. Silva, Mark Smith, Audrey Snider-Bell, Stocksnapper, tfjunction)

Library of Congress Cataloging-in-Publication Data

Frisch, Nate.
Yellowstone National Park / by Nate Frisch.
p. cm. — (Preserving America)
Includes bibliographical references and index.
Summary: An exploration of Yellowstone National Park, including how volcanoes helped form its landscape, its history of preservation, and tourist attractions such as the geyser called Old Faithful.

ISBN 978-1-60818-198-8
1. Yellowstone National Park—Juvenile literature. I. Title.
F722.F76 2013
978.7'52—dc23   2012023232

FIRST EDITION

2 4 6 8 9 7 5 3 1

Cover & page 3: *A bison grazing on a Yellowstone meadow; a bald eagle*

CREATIVE EDUCATION

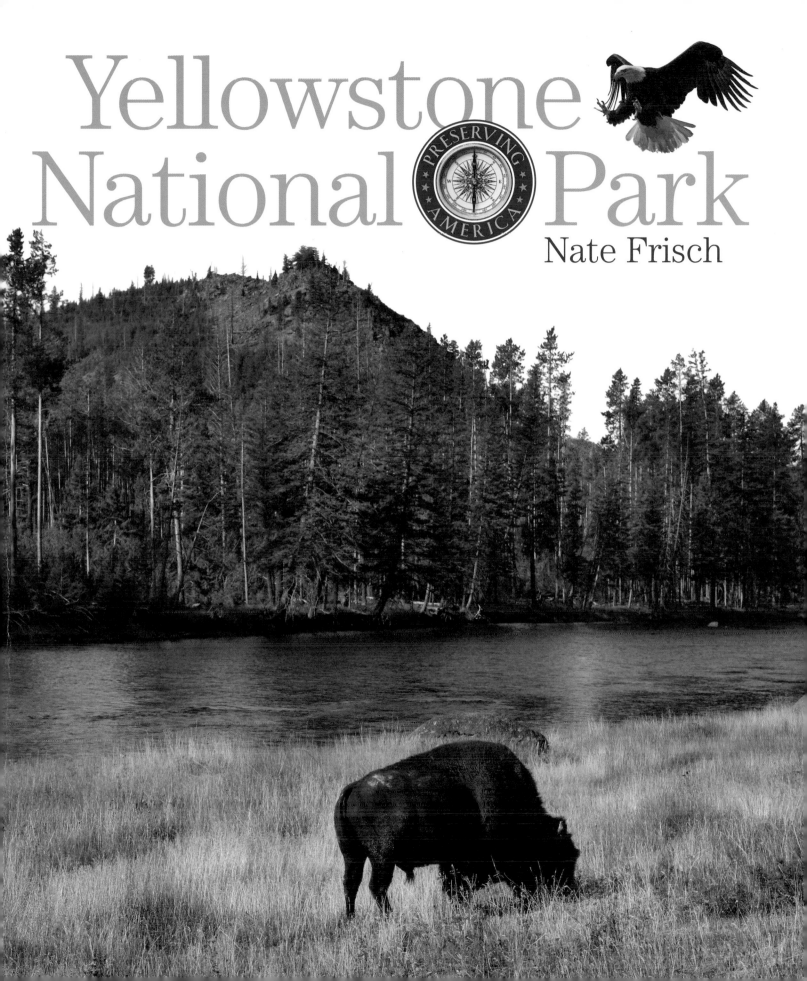

Yellowstone National Park

Nate Frisch

Table of Contents

TOWERING MOUNTAINS and glassy lakes. Churning rivers and dense forests. Lush prairies and baking deserts. The open spaces and natural wonders of the United States once seemed as limitless as they were diverse. But as human expansion and development increased in the 1800s, forests and prairies were replaced by settlements and agricultural lands. Waterways were diverted, wildlife was over-hunted, and the earth was scarred by mining. Fortunately, many Americans fought to preserve some of the country's vanishing wilderness. In 1872, Yellowstone National Park was established, becoming the first true national park in the world and paving the way for future preservation efforts. In 1901, Theodore Roosevelt became U.S. president. He once stated, "There can be no greater issue than that of conservation in this country," and during his presidency, Roosevelt signed five national parks into existence. The National Park Service (NPS) was created in 1916 to manage the growing number of U.S. parks. Nearly 60 American parks have come after Yellowstone National Park, but few offer the beauty and wildness of Yellowstone's mountain prairies, forests, and lakes, and none can come close to matching its geological marvels.

A Geological Wonderland

To look at Yellowstone National Park today, with its mature forests and imposing mountain ranges, it's hard to imagine the region ever being new. But until 2.1 million years ago, the entire area was beneath an expansive, shallow sea. Then the first of three major volcanic events took place. Hundreds of cubic miles of ash and volcanic rock erupted from the seabed, raising the land above the sea. About one million years later, lesser but still immensely powerful eruptions further altered the landscape.

The last major volcanic explosion occurred at Yellowstone about 640,000 years ago. Scientists believe it was an enormous blast—up to 100 times more powerful than the eruption that blew the top off Washington's Mount St. Helens in 1980. The eruption cracked the earth's crust, and vast amounts of ash and rock once again poured out, giving shape to the landforms visible in Yellowstone today.

Yellowstone's volcanic past is still evident. Within the current

Sitting atop a volcano, Yellowstone is a land of steam, with water heated underground creating various forms of hot springs

park boundaries lies the Yellowstone **Caldera**. The caldera, which was created by the last major eruption, covers more than 1,000 square miles (2,590 sq km) and, in fact, sits upon an older, larger caldera from a previous eruption. Volcanic rock is visible throughout the region, perhaps no more obviously than in Yellowstone's Obsidian Cliff. This wall of dark stone is composed of vertical columns that rise steeply from the prairie and tower over nearby pine forests. Obsidian, when cleaned and polished, is shiny black and has the texture of glass.

The most obvious reminder of the region's volcanic history is the **hydrothermal** activity that continues today. The park contains about 10,000 hydrothermal features, which is half of the total on Earth. These features take several different forms, but all share the basic ingredients of heat and groundwater. Molten rock is only a few miles below the Yellowstone Caldera, compared with the average distance of about 30

Grand Prismatic Spring is one of the most striking features in all of Yellowstone, as this hot spring showcases a dazzling array of colors

miles (48 km) below the earth's surface throughout the world's land regions. The ground around the caldera is also full of **fissures** and underground chambers. Rain or snow seeps in and, over time, heats up and rises to the surface. What form the hydrothermal features take depends on the amount of heat, water, and pressure involved.

The most common hydrothermal features in Yellowstone are hot springs. Many hot springs have enough water to form pools at the earth's surface. Yellowstone's largest pool, Grand Prismatic Spring, measures about 300 feet (91 m) by 250 feet (76 m) with a depth of 160 feet (49 m). The park's pools and the stone around them exhibit varying colors that are caused by the presence of minerals or microscopic organisms. Hot spring pools may boil or just ripple subtly as hot liquid continuously rises to the surface.

A less common example of a hot spring is exemplified by Yellowstone's Mammoth Hot Springs Terraces. In this case, instead of water rising through fissures in solid rock, it seeps through porous limestone. The water surfaces with little force but carries limestone particles above ground. These particles accumulate in layers, which then wear away at the edges as water runs off toward lower ground. The long-term result is otherworldly fountains from which water steadily trickles down tier after tier of bright white limestone.

Fumaroles are a type of hot spring with so little water that only steam and gases rise to the surface. The steam can attain temperatures

well above 200 °F (93 °C) and may create loud hissing sounds as it exits the earth. Yellowstone's Roaring Mountain, a hillside covered in fumaroles, was so named because it was particularly noisy years ago.

Mudpots are another type of hydrothermal feature with limited water. Underground, a gas called hydrogen sulfide mixes with hot water to form sulfuric acid, which dissolves some of the surrounding rock. In the case of Yellowstone's Fountain Paint Pot, the result is a thick, muddy mixture that bubbles and emits a potent "rotten egg" smell.

Perhaps the most impressive of all hydrothermal forms is the geyser. What makes geysers function differently from other features is the restriction of water as it rises to the surface. Narrow underground channels become temporarily sealed by mineral particles in the water, and pressure starts to build. When the gas and water pressure become too great, the seal bursts, and water erupts from the ground. The power, volume, and frequency of eruptions vary from geyser to geyser and even from eruption to eruption in the same geyser. Yellowstone's Steamboat Geyser can blast up to 300 feet (91 m) high. However, its eruptions are infrequent and are more commonly between 10 and 40 feet (3–12 km) high. True to its name, Old Faithful is generally consistent. While the time between eruptions does vary by up to an hour or more, the wait between one and the next rarely exceeds two hours. This frequency, combined with an impressive average height of almost 150 feet (46 m), has made Old Faithful a Yellowstone icon.

The majestic Yellowstone River and Grand Canyon of the Yellowstone make for views that have inspired many artists over the years

While hydrothermal features play a major role in defining Yellowstone, the region has many other diverse—if less rare—natural formations. The most obvious observation about Yellowstone is that it is mountainous, and the region's altitudes range from 5,282 feet (1,610 m) at Reese Creek to 11,358 feet (3,462 m) atop Eagle Peak. Most of Yellowstone's land is actually considered a **plateau**, and it is around its borders that more rugged mountain peaks and ranges exist.

Yellowstone features many lakes, rivers, and streams, the most prominent of which are Yellowstone Lake and Yellowstone River. Yellowstone Lake covers more than 135 square miles (350 sq km), with a maximum depth of 400 feet (122 m), and is the source of the Yellowstone River. Over thousands of years, the force of this river has carved the Grand Canyon of the Yellowstone. The canyon begins when the river abruptly plummets a combined 417 feet (127 m) over the course of 2 waterfalls: the Upper Falls and the larger Lower Falls. The high, steep canyon walls exhibit volcanic rock layers of bright yellow, orange, and red.

Yellowstone's biological wonders are as diverse as its geological features. In fact, Yellowstone is something of a living time capsule of native wildlife. Formerly widespread species such as bison and grizzly bears have been virtually erased from the U.S., but wild populations have always remained in Yellowstone. Other large species include elk, mule deer, black bears, moose, bighorn sheep, mountain goats, mountain lions, pronghorn, and wolves. The park also is home to an array of bird species that includes bald eagles, swans, geese, ducks, cranes, and many songbirds.

Supporting this amount and variety of animal life requires equally plentiful and varied plant life that can provide food and cover. Roughly three-fourths of the Yellowstone plateau is covered by forests, with the remaining portions being mostly prairie. The forests are dominated by hardy lodgepole pines. Stands of these **conifers** can be impressive in appearance and offer shelter but aren't a great food source. Instead, **herbivorous** animals seek out smaller **deciduous** trees, shrubs, and grasses. All told, Yellowstone contains more than 1,500 plant species, and mixed among the usual green and yellow leaves and grasses are wildflowers of many shapes and colors.

Because of its high elevation, Yellowstone has a rather cold climate. In midsummer, daily highs average a comfortable 78 °F (26 °C) at lower elevations, but overnight, temperatures can drop near or below the freezing point. Not surprisingly, winters can be bitterly cold, with daytime temperatures frequently dipping to 0 °F (-18 °C). Snow can fall at the region's highest altitudes year round, and snow cover across the park can be expected about half of the year.

Bison are an integral part of Yellowstone, as the park has always been a sanctuary for these animals that were once nearly wiped out

15

Keeping the West Wild

Evidence of human habitation in what is now the Yellowstone region of Wyoming, Montana, and Idaho dates back as far as 11,000 years. Early inhabitants were **nomadic** hunter-gatherers who followed the seasonal migration patterns of the wildlife they hunted. Within the past 1,000 years, tribes such as the Shoshone, Blackfeet, Crow, and Nez Perce hunted in and traveled through the area. Some Shoshone resided there permanently for a time.

Nestled in the Rocky Mountains, Yellowstone was not readily visible to or accessible by explorers. Among the first Europeans to investigate the area were fur trappers. In fact, they were likely responsible for the name "Yellowstone." The name was first applied to the Yellowstone River, which flows past yellow sandstone bluffs in eastern Montana. The river's source was later named Yellowstone Lake, and the surrounding areas became known as the Yellowstone region.

The first recorded venture into Yellowstone was that of John Colter, who arrived in 1807. Colter had journeyed to America's west coast with the famous Corps of Discovery expedition led by Meriwether Lewis and William Clark, but on the return trip toward St. Louis, Missouri, he left the party to pursue his own explorations. While his initial decision to stay behind had more to do with trapping than sightseeing, he was awestruck by the geysers and hydrothermal pools he encountered. Other trappers came in the years that followed. When they left Yellowstone, they took with them stories of steaming, alien landscapes that captivated readers and listeners back east.

This stamp commemorates the famed Lewis and Clark expedition, which brought some of the first white explorers to Yellowstone

In 1848, gold was found in California. During the gold craze that followed, most prospectors hurried to California, but some hoped to hit pay dirt in Yellowstone's mountains and rivers. Miners found little gold, but their tales of the region's incredible natural wonders reinforced what trappers had said years earlier and prompted new, more formal expeditions to make further discoveries.

From 1869 to 1871, three exploratory expeditions were launched into Yellowstone. The region was wild and rugged, and at times the parties endured bitter weather, became lost, and feared attack from American Indian tribes that were engaged in violent conflicts with the U.S. Army at the time. Overcoming these obstacles, the explorers created maps, made detailed notes of the landscape, and took measurements of waterfalls, trees, and mountains. The explorers also studied the hydrothermal features—naming Old Faithful in the process—and produced paintings and photographs of the various wonders of Yellowstone. These findings and images were soon published, validating many of the earlier trappers' and miners' seemingly far-fetched tales.

Public interest in Yellowstone grew, and members of the expeditions began lobbying the U.S. government to preserve Yellowstone under federal law. The influential Northern Pacific Railway company was quick to support the idea, as it was already building a railroad that would run near the Yellowstone region and envisioned the potential for big profits

The Shoshone, led by such famous figures as Chief Washakie (pictured), were a powerful Indian tribe in the Yellowstone area

from tourism. Some opposition arose from those who viewed Yellowstone as a prime source for logging, mining, and hunting, but because of the region's isolation, relatively few people used the land on a steady basis.

No national parks existed at that time, but several years earlier, president Abraham Lincoln had authorized the state of California to manage Yosemite Valley as a preserved park. That was not an option for Yellowstone, however, because Wyoming, Montana, and Idaho were **territories**—not states—at the time, and they lacked the authority and resources needed to manage a park. Having a park that existed in three separate territories at once complicated matters further.

Ultimately, the explorers' persuasive arguments, data, and images, along with Northern Pacific's backing, paid off. On March 1, 1872, president Ulysses S. Grant signed the Yellowstone National Park Act, creating the country's first federally managed park that was to be "dedicated and set apart as a public park or pleasuring-ground for the benefit and enjoyment of the people."

The new park was more or less rectangular in shape, measuring about 63 miles (101 km) from north to south and 54 miles (87 km) from east to west, and covering 3,472 square miles (8,992 sq km).

Its northern, southern, and western sides were mostly straight, artificial boundaries, while the irregular eastern border was determined by rivers and mountains. About 96 percent of the park lay within Wyoming, with the remaining portions contained in Montana and Idaho.

The official process by which Yellowstone became a national park had happened rather quickly, but plans that were easy to put on paper were more problematic in practice. The park was born during the "Old West" era, and many people—including veterans of the Civil War (1861–65)—were trying to eke out a living by any means possible. Regardless of laws created to protect the new park, Yellowstone was a land that many saw as ripe for hunting, trapping, mining, and logging, and there was little law enforcement out West to prevent such activities.

A member of two of the Yellowstone expeditions, Nathaniel Langford was the first man put in charge of park management. Unfortunately, he was provided with minimal funds and manpower and didn't even receive a salary. The park was initially expected to run on the funds brought in by tourism, but early on, few tourists came to the park, which lacked lodging or developed roads. Only about 300 visitors arrived in the park's first year. Without funds or staffing, Langford could do little to stop the poaching of animals and other prohibited activities.

In 1877, Yellowstone experienced perhaps its lowest point. The

Before receiving government protection, Yellowstone was viewed by some as a rich resource for harvesting animal furs and meat

park was struggling for funding, and that summer, a band of Nez Perce Indians was fleeing from U.S. Army soldiers tasked with forcibly relocating them to a reservation. The Indians entered Yellowstone, where they captured several tourists, killing two of them. Hoping to change the fortunes of the park, Yellowstone management replaced Langford as park supervisor that same year.

In the years that followed, the U.S. government began allocating more money to the park, allowing some of Yellowstone's earliest roads and facilities—such as a hotel near Mammoth Hot Springs—to be built. Park management also hired a designated gamekeeper to curb poaching and other exploitation of Yellowstone. Nearby tracks of the Northern Pacific railroad were completed in the early 1880s, and tourism increased sharply. However, Yellowstone was not yet protected or operated as its early proponents had envisioned, and in 1886, the federal government placed the park under the control of the U.S. Army.

The army ran Yellowstone for the next 30 years, during which time great progress was made toward making the park both lawful and accessible. The presence of soldiers deterred illegal activity in the park. Yellowstone's Grand Loop—the primary roadway still used today—was completed in 1915, and many of the park's most cherished buildings, such as Old Faithful Inn, were erected. In some ways, the military control seemed an odd fit, with soldiers acting as tour guides and game wardens. But ultimately, this multifaceted role as lawman, conservation officer, and park host created the mold for modern park rangers.

In the early 20th century, developments in transportation dramatically altered tourism. "Gateway" towns such as Cody (Wyoming), West Yellowstone (Montana), and Gardiner (Montana) had train depots by 1908, and soon tens of thousands of train passengers were arriving each year. The first automobiles rolled into Yellowstone in 1915, marking major changes in how visitors would experience the park, not to mention in the volume of visitors.

In 1916, a governmental branch called the National Park Service was created with the sole purpose of overseeing national parks and monuments. While Yellowstone fell under the NPS's jurisdiction, the army remained in the park for two more years to ease the transition. With these new shifts in park management and visitor access, Yellowstone entered its modern era.

Train travel helped open up the Yellowstone area— and the American West—as tracks were laid in the 1860s and '70s

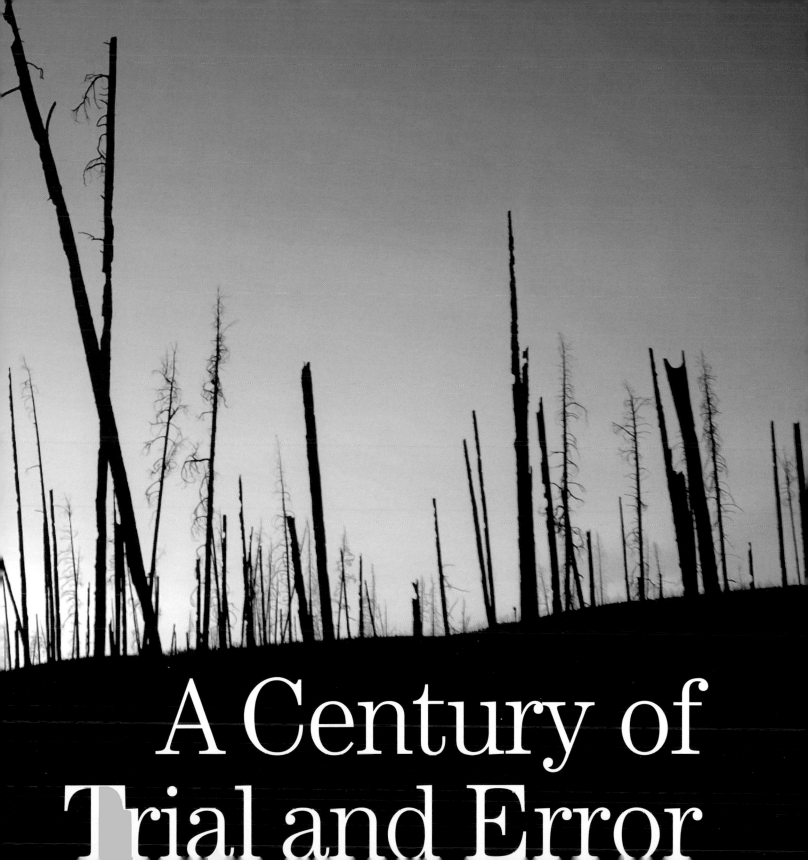

A Century of
Trial and Error

As the oldest national park in the world, Yellowstone has undergone much change over the course of 14 decades. Some alterations have occurred naturally, but many others resulted from human trial—and often error. Many such changes have revolved around the effort to strike a balance between Yellowstone the natural preserve and Yellowstone the tourist destination.

Since the park's early days, optimizing the populations of its many animal species has been a challenge. At the time the park was established, bison were nearly extinct, with unregulated slaughter having virtually eradicated the species. Herds that had once numbered 65 million had been reduced to under 1,000. In 1902, Yellowstone contained only 23 of the animals. What made Yellowstone's specimens particularly valuable was that they were genetically pure. Nearly all other bison in existence at that time were captive animals that contained traces of cattle **DNA**.

To ensure the survival and resurgence of Yellowstone's bison, park officials closely monitored the animals and provided them with hay to eat during the winter. Additional bison from domestic herds were also brought into the park. By 1954, about 1,500 bison lived in Yellowstone. Fearing that number was too large, park management decided to **cull** the herds, and only about 400 bison remained in the park by 1967. Shortly thereafter, park officials decided to let the bison live naturally without human control of herd size. The bison thrived, and by the 1990s, about 3,500 lived in Yellowstone.

As the free-roaming herds grew, more and more bison left Yellowstone's borders (especially to the north) in search of new grazing areas. Montana ranchers did not want bison wandering onto their land, where the animals could break fences, eat food intended for livestock, and potentially spread disease to domestic cattle. Park management

and the state of Montana developed policies that included herding bison deeper into the park and capturing bison that wandered out of Yellowstone. Population control policies were reenacted, with captured animals either being relocated in the park or slaughtered, depending on the current population and whether the bison carried disease. These practices remain in place today, and some bison within the park are culled as needed to maintain a population between 3,000 and 3,500.

Another Yellowstone trial-and-error process involved the park's buildings. When Old Faithful Inn was built in 1903, it was a huge and costly undertaking, but the end result was a landmark impressive enough to rival the park's natural attractions while still seeming in harmony with the Yellowstone wilderness. To this day, it is perhaps the most revered structure in the entire U.S. national park system. The inn's architect, Robert Reamer, went on to build or remodel four other Yellowstone hotels, each possessing a certain rustic charm.

However, starting in the late 1950s, Yellowstone made a push to

Accustomed to throngs of human visitors and vehicles, bison herds often assume control of the roadways in Yellowstone

update facilities and increase visitor capacity. In just a few years, cabins, a lodge, and a visitor center were erected, creating Yellowstone's Canyon Village. While the building designs were practical and cost-effective, they lacked any rustic appeal or personality, with interiors that resembled those of cheap motels. Many visitors saw this as an indication that park management was more concerned with increasing revenue than with enhancing the park experience. Since then, Canyon Village has been overhauled with remodeled or new buildings such as the Cascade and Dunraven lodges, which feature stone and timber accents and Western-themed furnishings.

Another controversial wildlife issue arose around 1914, when plans to increase Yellowstone's elk population went into effect. Those plans included killing wolves in the region, and by 1940, wolves had been **extirpated** from the park. Then, in the 1970s, talk began of reintroducing wolves because elk populations were *too* large. The strongest opposition came from nearby ranchers, who feared the wolves would leave the park and prey on livestock, and it wasn't until 1995 that reintroduction became a reality. Over the span of 2 years, 41 gray wolves from Canada were released in Yellowstone. Today, there are about 100 wolves in the park, and they have helped check inflated elk and coyote populations. This in turn has promoted the growth of vegetation that had long been overgrazed by the elk, as well as an increase in the fox population (competition with coyotes having reduced fox numbers previously). Still, for all its apparent success, the reintroduction of Yellowstone wolves remains a sore subject for area ranchers.

While the reintroduction of wolves in Yellowstone has been a long-running controversy, coyotes (pictured) have always been numerous

In a case in which tourism and nature conflicted, Fishing Bridge Visitor Center was built in 1931 along Yellowstone's east entrance road. The center was named after the bridge constructed at the site 29 years earlier, which crossed the Yellowstone River near

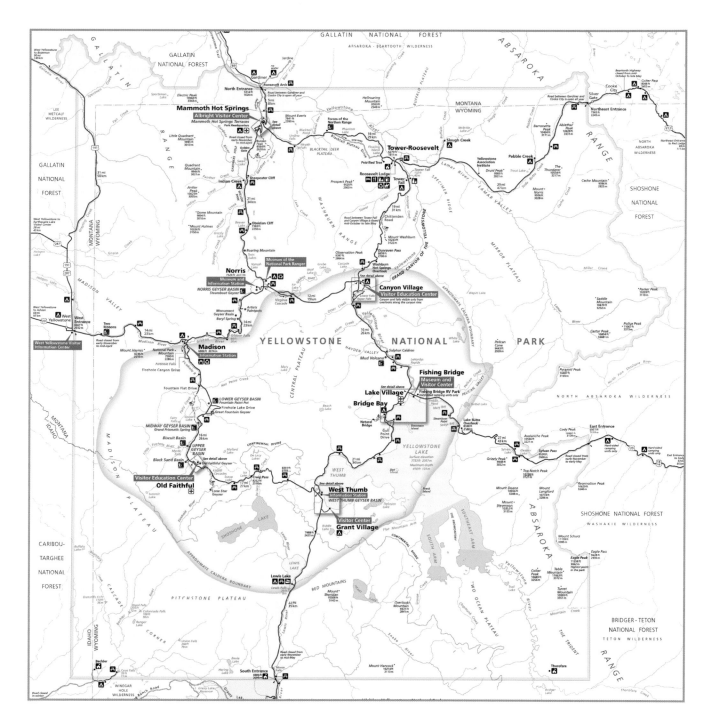

Yellowstone Lake. For decades, the area was popular among trout anglers and sightseers, but the human presence interfered with grizzly bear feeding areas near the water. The idea was eventually proposed that Fishing Bridge facilities be removed and replacements be built farther down the road. Yellowstone officials proceeded with the plan

This map illustrates Yellowstone National Park's centralized Grand Loop and the roads branching off toward park entrances

and, in the 1970s, built Grant Village several miles southwest of Fishing Bridge. However, Fishing Bridge was not scaled back as much as originally planned, and the newer Grant Village now infringed on a trout spawning area, which was also important habitat for grizzlies. Both sites remain in use today, but fishing has not been allowed at Fishing Bridge since 1973.

A drastic change to Yellowstone occurred in 1988 in the form of widespread forest fires. In previous years, naturally occurring wildfires were monitored but often allowed to burn themselves out, and **prescribed burns** were occasionally conducted as well. But the summer of 1988 turned out to be the driest in the park's history, and by July, multiple fires in the Yellowstone area had started either naturally or as the result of careless human behavior, and those fires raged with a rare intensity. The bone-dry needles and cones of lodgepole pines went up like tinder, while the branches and trunks of the trees provided long-lasting fuel. By the end of July, the fires were a national news story, with firefighters as well as U.S. Army and Marine units coming to the park in hopes of quelling the expanding blazes. Success was limited, however. Dry, windy conditions fanned the flames, and with few natural barriers or gaps in the forests, fires swept for miles across the park. While the efforts of more than 25,000 firefighters may have slowed the spread of the flames, it was September snowfalls that finally ended the blaze.

By the time the last spark died out, more than a third of Yellowstone—1,250 square miles (3,238 sq km)—had been burned, and 2 firefighters had been killed while battling flames outside the park. There were no fire-related deaths within park boundaries, and surprisingly few large animals died, but the flames destroyed 67 buildings throughout Yellowstone. During and after the threat, some people criticized park management, alleging that its initial response was too slow and allowed the situation to get out of control. Park officials contended that most of the damaging fires actually began outside the park. Regardless, Yellowstone and national parks across the country were forced to reevaluate their fire management policies. Today, stands of barren pine trunks can still be seen throughout the park, but new growth has long since sprouted from the nutrient-rich ashes.

Although wildfires have forever been part of the cycle of nature, they become big news when they threaten park structures

Something for Everyone

Today, Yellowstone draws more than 3 million visitors per year, and attendance is on the rise. Not surprisingly, the vast majority of visits take place during the summer, when Yellowstone is among the busiest parks in the country. Bookending the main tourist season, September and May are the fourth and fifth most popular months to visit Yellowstone. Attendance during the remaining seven months is low. There are about 10 times as many visitors from May to September as there are from October to April. Yellowstone attendance is particularly lopsided because of the park's chilly climate and high elevation. Mountain roads leading into the park show traces of snow even in midsummer, and most of them are closed completely from November through late March.

Yellowstone is relatively isolated, with no heavily populated regions nearby, so most visitors travel many miles to reach the park. Vehicle license plates from around the U.S. and Canada are seen in Yellowstone, and foreign tourists are common as well. Since people devote so much time to traveling to Yellowstone, they tend to stay a while once they arrive. Fortunately, the park offers more than enough sights and activities to fill several days or more.

There are about 600 grizzly bears in the Yellowstone area, though most visitors will never catch sight of one during their stay

Yellowstone can be appreciated in many ways, depending on each visitor's interests and time allotment. For those simply wanting to see the predominant features of the park, Yellowstone's Grand Loop Road leads guests directly to a wide variety of attractions, including various hydrothermal features, waterfalls, and access to Yellowstone Lake. The miles of road between the main attractions are dotted with miscellaneous points of interest and frequent pull-offs where visitors can take in views of the park's mountains, prairies, forests, and wildlife.

BEAR COUNTRY
Store all food in vehicle
Read bulletin board regulations
All wildlife are dangerous.

**REGISTER
BEFORE
ENTERING
CAMPGROUND**

Located near several of the prime attractions are park "villages" (eight in all) that feature picnic areas, restrooms, convenience stores, gift shops, restaurants, bus stops, museums, campgrounds, lodges, and cabins. The easy access to iconic natural features such as Old Faithful, Mammoth Hot Springs Terraces, and Lower Falls, plus the availability of some modern amenities, make Yellowstone a suitable destination for people who may not consider themselves "outdoorsy" but still want to take in the glory of one of America's great wilderness areas.

Yellowstone is also well suited to activity-oriented visitors who want to stretch their legs, pursue personal recreation, or get up-close to nature. The park has more than 1,100 miles (1,770 km) of hiking trails, and trail maps nicely break down those many miles into specific hikes that vary in difficulty, distance, and location. Hikers can determine in advance which trails will suit their fitness level, schedule, and scenery preferences. Yellowstone's concentration of impressive mammals, as well as its extensive bird list, add to the appeal of hiking the trails.

Yellowstone has more than 2,500 miles (4,023 km) of running water, 156 square miles (404 sq km) of lake surface, and several species of trout to entice anglers. The in-park fishing season runs from late March into early November, and permits are required for anglers 16 and older. Permits are also needed for visitors who bring their own boats. Guided boat trips and boat rentals are available at Yellowstone Lake, which is also the only lake in the park on which motorized boats are

With its waterways and woods, Yellowstone has a long-established reputation as one of America's classic outdoor getaways

permitted. Visitors with canoes or kayaks may prefer the calm and quiet of Shoshone, Lewis, or Heart lakes. Watercraft of any kind is prohibited on the park's rivers and streams.

Guided horseback rides are available in three different locations in Yellowstone. Most trips last one or two hours and are perfect for novice riders, as the horses are docile and the pace slow. Wagon rides are also available as an alternative to mounting a horse. For more advanced riders, horse trips involving **backcountry** camping can be arranged. Advance reservations are recommended for all rides.

Visitors can bring bicycles to Yellowstone or rent them within the park. This method of transportation allows tourists to not only cover a lot of ground but to take a pace with which they can be more aware of

Horseback riding is a unique way of seeing Yellowstone, as it combines scenic routes with a bit of Old West flair

the sights and sounds around them. Bicyclists can ride along most of the same routes that vehicles use, which include both paved and gravel roads. Bikes are not permitted on most hiking trails, however.

Yellowstone's mountains and cliffs offer rock climbers plenty of locations to pursue their hobby, though the park does not have any official climbing outfitters or services. Few written rules exist regarding the activity, so it is up to climbers themselves to take proper safety precautions and know their own capabilities.

Photographers and artists can find a virtually limitless array of worthy subjects in Yellowstone. Within the park's boundaries is a highly concentrated assortment of natural features and wildlife, including some that are found nowhere else in the world. Add to that Yellowstone's four

distinct changes of season, and there is no shortage of inspiring imagery.

The relatively rare visitor who comes during Yellowstone's snowy months is treated to a unique perspective of the park. Bison and elk stand out in sharp contrast against the brilliantly white winterscapes, and especially thick columns of steam continuously rise from the geyser basins and hot springs. The winter months allow for seasonal activities such as cross-country skiing and snowmobiling. Snowmobiles, whether brought in or rented, are generally limited to park roadways, but the park is a giant wintry playground for cross-country skiers, who are much less restricted.

Because summer attendance is so high and guests tend to stay for at least several days, Yellowstone offers several types of overnight accommodation. Options range from contemporary hotels to backcountry camping, with many other options falling somewhere in between, including modern and rustic inns and cabins, RV/trailer camping, and drive-in tenting.

Obtaining accommodations in Yellowstone's most popular lodges often requires reservations made a year or more in advance, and no lodge is more popular or impressive than Old Faithful Inn. This seven-story, pitched-roof lodge is constructed primarily from huge timbers, with stone and wrought-iron accents adding to its rustic appeal. Visitors often step inside Old Faithful Inn just to view its main hall, which, as its center point, features an enormous stone fireplace reaching up to the 90-foot (27 m) ceiling. Wooden pillars support tiers of balconies that surround the main hall and offer plenty of sitting space for those wanting to enjoy the warm ambience of the inn.

Winter is a challenge for most Yellowstone animals, but with the arrival of spring, the land turns green and bountiful once again

All told, Yellowstone has more than 2,100 inn or hotel rooms and cabins available during the busy summer season. Campers, meanwhile,

The famous Old Faithful Inn (right) affords very comfortable lodging in the middle of this spectacular land of bears and geysers

have 12 campgrounds and more than 2,000 campsites from which to choose. The five largest campgrounds accept reservations, while the seven smaller campgrounds operate on a first-come, first-served basis. Most campgrounds accommodate both RVs and tents, but Fishing Bridge RV Park, on Yellowstone's eastern side, does not permit tenting because of the high frequency of local bear activity. Bears may actually be anywhere in the park, so all campgrounds have large, metal, bear-proof boxes in which visitors can secure food.

Yellowstone's larger campgrounds provide access to showers, laundry, and restrooms with modern plumbing. Smaller campgrounds have only primitive toilets, and campers must go to one of the park's designated shower/laundry locations for those luxuries. Campsites throughout the park have fire rings, and fires may not be built anywhere else. Visitors wanting a wilder and more isolated experience can acquire a permit to camp in one of Yellowstone's backcountry sites.

The visitor experience at Yellowstone today is far different from that of the park's earliest tourists. Changes made over the years to accommodate more guests have made Yellowstone accessible to many types of people, but that has led to bigger crowds and some less-than-natural guardrails, walkways, and facilities. Nonetheless, the vast majority of Yellowstone National Park remains as timeless as ever—a rugged wilderness of mountains, rising steam, forests, and wildlife matched nowhere else on Earth.

A threatened species just a few decades ago, the bald eagle has made a triumphant return in Yellowstone and beyond

Giant of the Prairie

Weighing up to a ton (910 kg) or more, American plains bison—commonly called buffalo—are imposing creatures with massive heads, powerful shoulders, and stout horns. Bison can be seen throughout much of Yellowstone but tend to favor open prairies, where they feed. Males, called bulls, are commonly seen alone or in small groups, while cows and young bison typically stay with a herd. Bison often seem unwary of humans and will leisurely stroll along roadways. This behavior can be misleading, however. Yellowstone's bison are wild and unpredictable animals that can sprint up to 35 miles (56 km) per hour. Each year, more Yellowstone visitors are injured by bison than by bears.

Yellowstone's Heart-Stopper

Perhaps no animal in Yellowstone sparks the imagination as much as the grizzly bear. Whether hoping to catch a glimpse of one from a road-way or hoping to avoid one on a hike, many visitors have grizzlies on their minds during their stay in the park. Weighing up to 800 pounds (363 kg), grizzly bears are fast and powerful enough to kill bison

*and elk yet nimble enough to pluck trout from a stream. As **omnivores**, they actually get most of their meals from grasses, leaves, and berries. Grizzlies once inhabited about half of the U.S. Now Yellowstone is among the few places in the country where wild grizzlies exist.*

Old Yellow Bus Tours

A great option for Yellowstone visitors on a limited schedule is an Old Yellow Bus tour. As the name suggests, the buses used are, in fact, old (some of them were built in the 1930s) and yellow. They were retired from service for 50 years until 2007, when they were refurbished and put back into action, providing guests with a throwback sightseeing experience. The buses feature large, open-air windows and allow visitors to sit back comfortably while gazing at some of the park's most impressive sights and wildlife. Onboard tour guides provide light-hearted but insightful commentary about the park and its history.

Yellowstone Hide-and-Seek

Although Yellowstone is home to many animals, visitors have no guarantee of spotting the more reclusive species. Those wanting to

increase their odds often head for Lamar Valley along the northeast entrance road. Dawn and dusk are the best times for glimpsing wolves or bears, while bison and elk can be seen throughout the day. There are several pull-offs along the road for wildlife viewing, but visitors feeling more adventurous can hike the Lamar Valley Trail. It's more than five miles (8 km) one way and includes multiple stream crossings, but those who are up to it may be rewarded with a wolf sighting.

A Scenic Neighbor

Just a few miles south of Yellowstone's border is Grand Teton National Park. Named for the Teton Range found within the park, Grand Teton lacks the hydrothermal features of its more popular northern neighbor but makes up for this with perhaps the most impressive mountainscapes in America. The sharply defined Teton Range lies along the western edge of the park and is particularly impressive when reflecting sunlight from the east. Grand Teton's Jenny Lake, at the eastern foot of the mountains, is a popular destination for hikers or anyone wanting to view calendar-worthy scenery.

Reliving the Old West

About an hour's drive east of Yellowstone lies the town of Cody, Wyoming. Named after hunter and Western showman "Buffalo Bill" Cody, who was instrumental in the town's founding, Cody offers visitors

some Old West atmosphere in the form of historic buildings, Western shops and museums, and a large rodeo arena. The "Cody Nite Rodeo" is held every night in June, July, and August and has been running for more than 55 years, earning Cody the title of "Rodeo Capital of the World." The town's numerous modern establishments may compromise a true 19th-century experience, but Cody's longstanding attractions still give visitors a taste of that bygone era.

Hiking in Bear Country

The knowledge that bears are out and about can deter some hikers in Yellowstone. Fortunately, bears tend to avoid humans and typically show aggression only when surprised at close range. Therefore, hikers are encouraged to make noise while walking so bears are not caught unaware. Many people attach small bells to their clothing or walking stick for this reason. Also, because bears are less likely to be aggressive toward multiple people, hiking in groups is recommended. As a last line of defense, bear spray— essentially an oversized can of pepper spray—has proven effective in repelling bear attacks.

Keeping Safe in the Cold

Hypothermia occurs when a person's body temperature drops below 95 °F (35 °C). Symptoms range from shivering to impaired body and brain function, and in extreme cases, the condition can be fatal. Hypothermia is primarily caused by exposure to cold air or—worse—cold water. Yellowstone's air temperatures can dip to freezing, even in summer, and its lakes and streams are cold year round. Hikers and boaters are well advised to keep dry, insulated clothing on hand and to dress in

layers with a weather-resistant layer on the outside. Hypothermia victims stuck outdoors should be kept dry and sheltered from the wind. Building a fire, drinking warm liquids, and sharing body heat can all help remedy the condition until further help can be sought.

Glossary

backcountry: an area that is away from developed or populated areas

caldera: a broad, craterlike basin of a volcano, formed by the collapse of the volcanic cone following a major eruption

conifers: trees or shrubs usually having needle-shaped or scalelike leaves and seed-producing cones

cull: to reduce or control the size of an animal herd by removal or killing certain animals

deciduous: describing plants that shed their leaves in the fall

DNA: the abbreviation for "deoxyribonucleic acid," a substance found in all organisms that carries genetic information

extirpated: destroyed or removed completely

fissures: long, deep, narrow openings or cracks in the earth

herbivorous: describing animals that feed mostly or exclusively on plants

hydrothermal: relating to the action of hot underground water in producing minerals and springs

nomadic: describing people who move frequently to new locations in order to obtain food, water, and shelter

omnivores: animals that eat many sorts of food, including both plants and other animals

plateau: an area of high ground with a fairly level surface

prescribed burns: fires that are intentionally ignited and contained within a designated area as a means of reducing fire hazards or promoting new plant growth

territories: areas of the U.S. that fall under control of the American government but do not have the classification of states

Selected Bibliography

Bauer, Erwin A. *Yellowstone*. Stillwater, Minn.: Voyageur Press, 1993.

Cahill, Tim. *Lost in My Own Backyard: A Walk in Yellowstone National Park*. New York: Crown Journeys, 2004.

Kevin, Brian. *Yellowstone and Grand Teton National Parks*. New York: Random House, 2009.

Meyer, Judith L. *The Spirit of Yellowstone: The Cultural Evolution of a National Park*. Lanham, Md.: Rowman & Littlefield, 1996.

National Geographic Guide to the National Parks of the United States. Washington, D.C.: National Geographic Society, 2009.

Schullery, Paul. *America's National Parks: The Spectacular Forces That Shaped Our Treasured Lands*. New York: DK Publishing, 2001.

White, Mel. *Complete National Parks of the United States*. Washington, D.C.: National Geographic Society, 2009.

Websites

National Geographic: Yellowstone National Park
http://travel.nationalgeographic.com/travel/national-parks/yellowstone-national-park/
This site provides a concise visitor's guide to Yellowstone, complete with maps, photos, sightseeing suggestions, and links to other popular national parks.

Yellowstone National Park
http://www.nps.gov/yell/index.htm
The official National Park Service site for Yellowstone is the most complete online source for information on the park and includes live videos of Yellowstone geysers.

Index